How to Write a School Development Plan

How to Write a School Development Plan

Devised, piloted and written by the Staff of Norham Community High School

Supported by the WHOLE CURRICULUM ISSUES PROJECT TEAM

Les Walton (Headteacher, Norham Community High School)
Allan Foster (WCIP Project Manager)
Bruce Gillham (TVEI/ITT Co-ordinator, University of Northumbria at Newcastle)
Diane Greaves (Adviser, North Tyneside LEA)
Peter Parish (North Tyneside TVEI Co-ordinator)
Ken Shenton (North East Educational Management Unit)

Edited by Rick Rogers

Heinemann

How to Write a School Development Plan

Heinemann Educational
a division of Heinemann Publishers (Oxford) Ltd.,
Halley Court, Jordan Hill, Oxford OX2 8EJ

OXFORD   LONDON   EDINBURGH
MADRID   ATHENS   BOLOGNA   PARIS
MELBOURNE   SYDNEY   AUCKLAND   SINGAPORE
TOKYO   IBADAN   NAIROBI   HARARE   GABORONE
PORTSMOUTH NH (USA)

First published 1994

A catalogue record for this book is available from the British Library

ISBN 0 435 800450

94 95 96 97 98

9 8 7 6 5 4 3 2

Designed by Gecko Limited, Bicester, Oxon
Printed by Athenæum Press Limited, Newcastle-upon-Tyne

Contents

Developmental planning explained

Introduction

We plan to achieve our dreams and, as teachers and heads, some of us dream of being able to plan. There is no one way to organize a school and no single management ethos which is best for all schools. However, to plan successfully, every school must have answers to four basic questions:

- Where is the school now?
- What changes are needed?
- How can we manage those changes?
- How do we know that we are being successful?

Developmental planning enables a school to provide answers to these questions. It is

- a particular way of planning geared towards creating development and change in the school;
- concerned with what is happening now and what can be made to happen in the future;
- aimed at creating coherence and directing purpose.

Developmental planning has long been used throughout business and industry. It is now spreading into schools and colleges, where resistance to the use of management techniques is fast breaking down. Their value lies, as many schools are discovering, in being able to help manage a better-run school that meets the goals it sets itself without compromising its own ethos.

Many teachers want a practical and manageable approach to developmental planning which will simplify – and at the same time enrich – their own experience of the school management process. This guide has been specifically designed for that purpose, by teachers, for teachers.

Since developmental planning should embrace other groups involved in the school, the needs of governors, parents, employers and pupils were also kept in mind during the compilation of this guide. They have since used and benefited from the materials provided. Other agencies, too, have made use of the materials, including local businesses, health authorities and police authorities. They certainly, therefore, have a universal application.

If you need any further advice or would like to discuss this guide, contact the WCIP Project Manager, Norham Community High School, Alnwick Avenue, North Shields NE29 7BU; telephone 091 257 6131.

Developmental planning is both

a *planning procedure*
- geared towards development and change, and
- concerned with the present and the future;

and a *management tool*
- aimed at coherence and purpose.

Developmental planning

What is developmental planning? How can it benefit your school? It obviously means having a plan to which everyone can refer and to find their agreed route ahead, like an Ordnance Survey map. But it is more than this. It is a way of thinking and acting across all areas of the school.

Developmental planning is a process or activity which affects – and can enhance – the whole school and everything it does. This process enables a school to organize what it is already doing and what it needs to do in a more purposeful and coherent way.

The Department for Education describes developmental planning as follows:

'A school development plan is a plan of needs for development set in the context of the school's aims and values, its existing achievements and national and LEA policies and initiatives ... The purpose of development planning is to assist the school to introduce changes successfully, so that the quality of teaching and standards of learning are improved. It does so by creating the conditions under which innovations, such as the National Curriculum, can be successfully introduced.'

However, although developmental planning is becoming more widely accepted, we have found that most of the models being offered for schools to follow are too prescriptive – for example, every school is expected to start at the same place and follow a rigid sequence of steps.

Furthermore, many schools are finding that planning is not the simple task which many experts originally claimed it to be. For example, one local authority cited the following difficulties:

- the regular developmental planning cycle 'rarely works as smoothly as might be expected from reading some of the guidance material that is available – key staff are absent, deadlines are missed, decisions take longer than expected, and the timetable for the plan slips';
- the development plan is 'very different in different schools at different times'. The scope of activity varies greatly – from a major piece of work to a few running repairs.

The local authority describes one headteacher's experience as no longer seeing the plan as a 'report' but as a loose-leaf folder that is continually updated.

Another identified 'variation' from the norm which so many model plans offer is how a school views the purpose of developmental planning. This is sometimes an either/or situation, for example:

- guiding the school into the future, or increasing awareness of where it is now;
- developing fresh initiatives, or listing current commitments;
- promoting change, or achieving consensus;
- a manifesto, or a reference document.

Of course, some schools pursue some, or even all, of these purposes together or at different times, also setting them in order of priority – which, in turn, changes.

The local authority also found that some schools limited the written plan to whole-school issues; others brought together individual departmental reports; while a few did both. All this highlights the variety of schools' needs when it comes to developmental planning. Here, therefore, a more flexible approach is offered, which can be adapted to a school's own situation and experience. The needs of people, rather than a formula, have been the focus point for this guide.

The advantages

The point of developmental planning is that it should give you what you want. Here are some of the advantages to be gained. Which ones are useful to you?

Advantage	You can:	Tick if this is useful for you/ your staff
Accountability	Ensure accountability and be confident of the appraisal process.	
Clarity	Think through the issues without losing sight of the main purpose.	
Communication	Share ideas and plans.	
Control	Feel and *be* in control, and so reduce stress.	
Co-operation	Build a team to work amicably together.	
Flexibility	Adapt the plan to any level or situation, and react readily to changes.	
Focus	Focus your aims and always know where you are going.	
Integration	Integrate planning into the school and oversee the development of the school as a whole.	
Organization	Organize your actions, work through the logical sequence of events and plan for the future.	
Priority	Identify your priorities and concentrate on the important things for your school.	
Reporting	Devise an effective framework for reporting.	
Speed	Respond quickly and rationally to current demands.	
Staff development	Help staff gain new skills and knowledge.	

Our model

Here is a diagrammatic representation of a model for developmental planning.

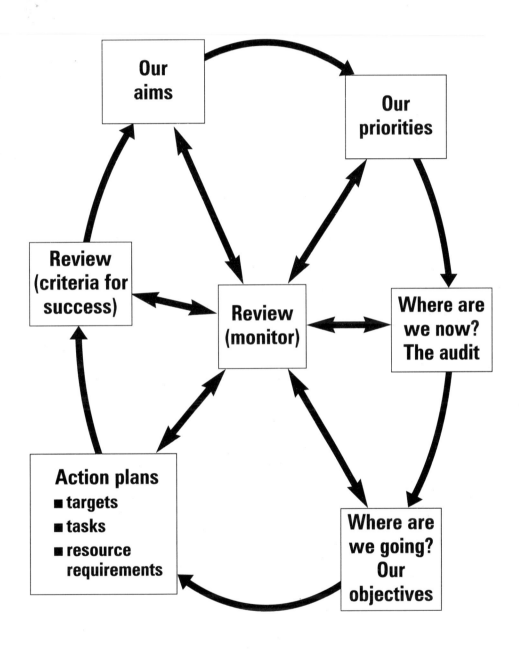

An explanation of the terminology used in this diagram is given on the following page.

Definitions and interpretations

The terms used in this model have a range of definitions and interpretations. Below is explained what is meant by them. Space is provided for you to write down your responses and observations. These are not put forward as a rigid set of definitions. Your own comments on and extensions of these terms and ideas are an essential part of getting involved with the model. Our definitions are a useful management approach which you need to make your own.

Development plan
A map of the most suitable route to get to where the school, or department, wants to be.

Aims
The long-term goals, based on the school's values and philosophy, which transcend all other, shorter-term or minor goals.

Priority
Giving greater or lesser weight to specific aims over the period for which you are planning.

Audit
A way to describe, record and understand the current situation using a variety of techniques.

Objectives
Precise and measurable statements of intended outcomes which specify intentions rather than actions.

Action plan
A programme which sets out targets and tasks designed to help you achieve your objectives.

Target
A timed element within the programme.

Task
A specific job to be carried out within the time imposed by the target.

Resource
Material and support which generates a cost in terms of time, human energy or other materials.

Review (monitor)
A continuous process of examining the emerging results of the plan as it is being carried out.

Review (criteria for success)
An end-of-process review leading to the next development cycle.

The principles involved

Four principles underpin the planning model:

> 1 **You can start at any point.**
> 2 **Monitoring is placed at the heart of the process.**
> 3 **You can plan at a variety of levels using the same process.**
> 4 **You can use the model for a range of purposes in many different enterprises.**

This model has been designed to be highly flexible, adaptable and non-specific so that it can deal with the dynamic and ever-changing situations which managers in education now face.

Principle 1

The opportunity to start anywhere in the model allows you to recognize the point you have currently reached and the work you have already completed. It also enables you to make the decisions about what is needed and how you should proceed. Prescription and close control have been avoided so that, within the framework of the model, you have the freedom to make the running.

Principle 2

With monitoring – review (monitor) – at the centre of the model you can, almost constantly, assess your progress and slip from one part of the model to another. For example, you may start with an **Audit**, but find that on reviewing the evidence your overall aims remain unclear. The model enables you to switch across to a reconsideration of your **Aims**.

Principle 3

The multi-level nature of the model means you can use it throughout the school, for example

- at whole-school level: to develop and operate the framework for a whole-school policy;
- at departmental level: to plan as a team for curriculum innovation which requires a rapid response;
- at classroom level: to decide on and design a teacher's personal response to classroom management.
- at pupil level: to help children work on their own personal action and development plans.

Principle 4

The universality of the model – in being suitable for use across the education sectors and for different purposes – has meant that it is already being applied to a range of activities from project management to training students for entry to the teaching profession.

Using the technique

To ease you in gently, a simple proforma built around the model has been devised. There is nothing magical about this proforma. You can go on to design one which best fits your own situation.

| TITLE _____ |
| MANAGER _____ DATE _____ |

Our aims	**Where are we now?**	**Action plans**	
		Target and date:	Target and date:
		Tasks:	Tasks:
		Resources required:	Resources required:
		Criteria for success:	Criteria for success:
Our priorities	**Where are we going?**		

On the next page is what this sort of proforma looks like when it has been used, in this case by a team of teachers involved in developing Health Education.

TITLE: *Health Education*
MANAGER: *Mr T D Lewis*

DATE: *14th December*

Our aims

1 To provide facilities which enable children to follow a healthy lifestyle in school.
2 To develop a whole-school approach towards Health Education within and outside the structured curriculum.
3 To promote an environment which is sensitive and responsive to the emotional needs of children.
4 To promote knowledge and understanding of factors affecting physical health.
5 To develop understanding of the needs of others and to foster responsible and caring attitudes towards others.
6 To promote environmental awareness and to assist in responding to community needs.

Where are we now?

1 Health Education topics are being addressed in a number of curriculum areas but with no cross-curricular co-ordination of content, context, timing or use of resources.
2 There have been few whole-school activities specifically planned to promote Health Education.
3 North Tyneside LEA has issued a Health Education Policy and guidelines.
4 HMIs have issued recommendation for cross-curricular Health Education (Curriculum Matters Series).
5 Individuals have expressed concern for the unhealthy diet of many pupils at lunchtime.

Action plans

Target one
Date: 7th March

To negotiate a school Health Education Policy which meets the approval of teachers, governors and the LEA.

Tasks:
1 Analysis of LEA and HMI recommendations.
2 Identify Statements of Attainment related to Health Education (Science NC).
3 Circulate draft policy for whole school discussion and feedback.
4 Prepare final draft policy.
5 Agenda policy for approval at governors' meeting.

Resources:
1 Duplication of initial draft and final draft policies.
2 Meeting time for discussion at department, canton and whole staff, and governors' meetings.
3 LEA, HMI and National Curriculum documentation.

Criteria for success:
Final policy for Health Education within the school is approved by staff, governors and LEA.

Target two
Date: 12th April

To organize a whole school 'Healthy Eating Week' (12th–16th March).
To include:
■ a new school menu;
■ a re-arrangement of the dining room and its procedures;
■ an awareness-raising with pupils, parents and staff;
■ a curricular contribution from departments to the theme of the week.

Tasks:
1 Arrange meeting with head school meals adviser, cook and other staff, to discuss menus.
2 Review dining room arrangements and procedures.
3 Prepare campaign booklets.
4 Request department inputs.
5 Publicity in schools and social press.
6 Organize competition for pupils.
7 Produce programme of related activities.

Resources:
1 Meeting time for task one.
2 Materials for booklets, posters, badges etc.
3 Time for preparation of tasks 3, 5 and 7.
4 Assembly time for awareness-raising.

Criteria for success:
Results of competition and observation indicate that children are choosing a healthier diet. New arrangements meet with pupils' and staff approval.

Our priorities

1 To negotiate a school HEALTH EDUCATION POLICY.
2 To provide facilities to encourage children to choose a healthy diet in school.
3 To explore the extent to which HEALTH EDUCATION topics are presently being addressed within the structured curriculum.

Where are we going?

1 A school Health Education Policy is to be developed by the Science and Health Canton, in negotiation with the Headteacher, Governors, LEA Adviser and all staff.
2 A 'just a tick' audit of Health Education topics presently being addressed within the structured curriculum is to be made throughout all cantons.
3 A more detailed audit of topics will then follow to analyse content, teaching methods, terms taught and resources used for each year group in Health Education.
4 Present Health Education provision will be reviewed in its effectiveness to meet the policy aims of the school.
5 Inadequacies and duplication within Health Education topics will be addressed within priorities.
6 School meals will be improved in dietary balance and the dining room environment will be improved.

2 Your aims: what do you value most?

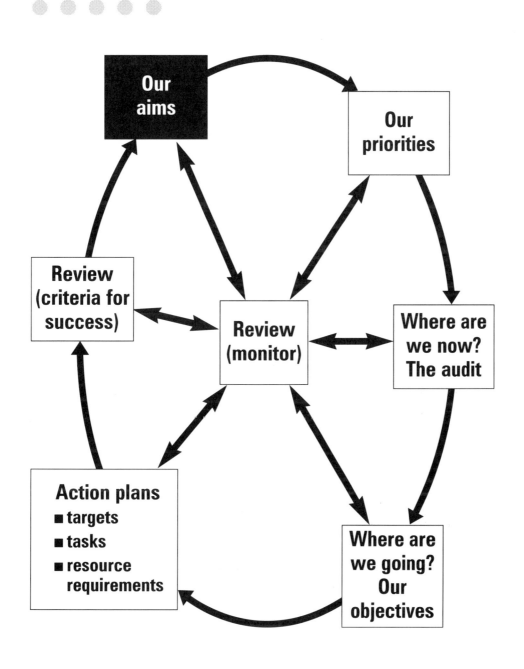

- Our aims
- Our priorities
- Review (criteria for success)
- Review (monitor)
- Where are we now? The audit
- Action plans
  - targets
  - tasks
  - resource requirements
- Where are we going? Our objectives

This is where you begin work on the development plan. Your aim is to ensure that you are clear on what you are doing and why you are doing it. You are also shown how to bring together everyone involved as a team for developing and carrying through the plan. Here the following are considered:

■ Defining aims: what do you value most?
■ Agreeing priorities: what are the urgent tasks?
■ Carrying out an audit: where are you now?
■ Setting objectives: where are you going?

What is an aim?

An aim is a long-term goal which transcends other, minor goals. The aims of a school are about values and philosophy, and are underpinned by statements which clearly show the vision and aspirations of:

■ the individual;
■ the group;
■ the organization.

For example:

> **'All children shall be treated equally, regardless of their colour, class or creed.'**
> **'All children have the potential to achieve more.'**
> **'Children must always be at the centre of our decision-making process.'**

All organizations should have clearly stated aims. For example, take the aims of three different schools.

School one: to operate procedures which are smooth and efficient.
School two: to relate the curriculum to the world of work.
School three: to develop in pupils the qualities of mind, body, spirit, feelings and imagination.

What are the values and beliefs which underpin the above aims?

School one
This school values:

School two
This school values:

School three
This school values:

Thinking carefully about your aims

You can plan better if you identify and understand the different sorts of aims. For example, consider these five aims and the questions asked about them:

AIMS	QUESTIONS
To develop mathematical knowledge which encourages confidence and produces success.	Is this aim serving the needs of the whole society or just a particular group?
To enable pupils with special educational needs to fulfil their potential.	Is this aim concerned with the special educational needs process or output?
To develop a staffing structure which is responsive to change.	Is this aim concerned with the structural needs of the school or the developmental needs of the teachers?
To equip pupils for working life.	Does this aim emphasize the process of developing children or the product?
To care for and serve the needs of the local community.	Is this aim central to the school or is it pursuing other goals outside the school?

Think about your aims in this way and devise your own aims statement.

For an example, look at the aims of National Curriculum Citizenship.

The aims of education for citizenship are to:
■ *establish the importance of positive, participative citizenship and provide the motivation to join in*

and

■ *help pupils to acquire and understand essential information on which to base the development of their skills, values and attitudes towards citizenship.*

Curriculum Guidance 3: The Whole Curriculum (page 5)

Look at these aims and use the checklist:

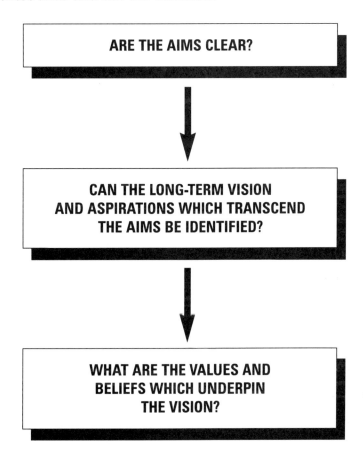

ARE THE AIMS CLEAR?

CAN THE LONG-TERM VISION AND ASPIRATIONS WHICH TRANSCEND THE AIMS BE IDENTIFIED?

WHAT ARE THE VALUES AND BELIEFS WHICH UNDERPIN THE VISION?

Using an aims statement

Devising an aims statement is a valuable exercise in itself. It helps you to work out where you are and what directions to go in. But it is also an essential ingredient in formulating strategies. Below is an example of an aims/strategy grid linked to a *School Means Business* plan.

'SCHOOL MEANS BUSINESS' (COMPACT) AIMS STATEMENT	**Aim one** **Partnership**: to bring education and industry together; to increase mutual understanding and respect.
Strategy one	Seeking additional support skills and resources.
Strategy two	Providing industrial placement.
Strategy three	Providing access for employers to a better motivated school leaver.
Strategy four	Involving parents.
Strategy five	Raising awareness of the project to external groups.
Strategy six	
Strategy seven	
Strategy eight	
Strategy nine	
Strategy ten	
Strategy eleven	
Strategy twelve	

Aim two **Prospects:** to increase students' prospects in work, FE and in the community in which they live.	Aim three **Potential:** to develop personal, social and academic skills; to increase student motivation; to enhance and enrich the curriculum.
Providing quality training and worthwhile job opportunities.	Raising levels of achievement.
Raising realistic expectations.	Empowering and involving students.
Preparing young people for working life.	Developing initiative.
Developing social skills needed in existing and emerging industries, bearing in mind the need for a broad and balanced curriculum.	Raising self-esteem.
Preparing young people to participate in the community in which they live.	Promoting equal opportunites.
Making young people aware of demographic changes.	Providing more careers guidance and counselling.
Contributing to the regeneration of the community.	Introducing targets eg, attendance, punctuality, course completion.
Encouraging more people to progress to further and higher education.	Giving students a broad education relevant to their future lives.
	Developing keyboard skills and IT.
	Raising standards of literacy and numeracy.
	Increasing levels of achievement in technology.
	Introducing a European dimension to prepare pupils for the EC.

On the following pages you will find a blank aims/strategy grid for you
to practise on.

A blank grid to work on

Title of development plan:	Aim one
Strategy one	
Strategy two	
Strategy three	
Strategy four	
Strategy five	
Strategy six	
Strategy seven	
Strategy eight	
Strategy nine	
Strategy ten	
Strategy eleven	
Strategy twelve	

Aim two	Aim three

Aim four	Aim five

Aim six	Aim seven

3 *Your priorities: what is most important?*

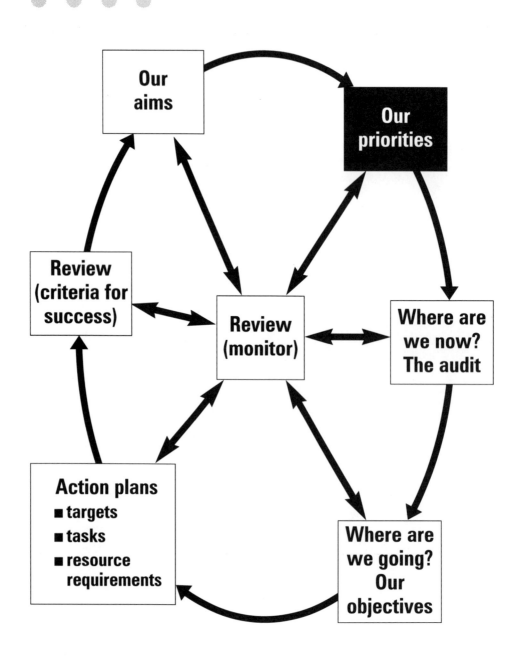

Our aims

Our priorities

Review (criteria for success)

Review (monitor)

Where are we now? The audit

Action plans
■ targets
■ tasks
■ resource requirements

Where are we going? Our objectives

What is a priority?

A priority means giving greater or lesser weight to particular aims. Setting priorities is important because

■ you can't do everything at once;
■ you work with scarce resources: people, time, skills, materials.

People have different priorities. How do you resolve the differences?

Priorities matter at all levels and in all areas

The effective teacher-manager can deal successfully with a wide range of issues by setting priorities.

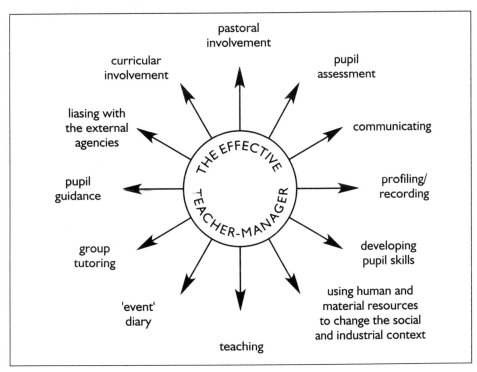

If you do not set priorities, you can feel overwhelmed by the number of options open to you.

Paired comparisons

A useful technique to adopt if other people are involved in setting priorities is 'paired comparisons'. This is how it works:

- Construct a grid like the one below.
- List your objectives down the left-hand side of the grid.
- Take the first objective and compare it with the second. Which is more important to you? If it is the second one, circle the '2'.
- Then compare objective 1 with objectives 3, 4, and so on.
- When you have completed all the comparisons with objective 1, do the same for objective 2, then objective 3, and so on.
- When you have finished, add up the number of 1s, 2s, and so on, which you have circled. You should then be able to list your aims in order of priority.

OBJECTIVE						TOTAL	RANK ORDER
1	1 / 2	1 / 3	1 / 4	1 / 5	1 / 6	☐ 1	
2	2 / 3	2 / 4	2 / 5	2 / 6		☐ 2	
3	3 / 4	3 / 5	3 / 6			☐ 3	
4	4 / 5	4 / 6				☐ 4	
5	5 / 6					☐ 5	
6						☐ 6	

This technique enables you to rank priorities in a more ordered way and is useful in reaching shared priorities with a group of people.

Setting priorities

How will you set the priorities for your school? By imposing your own, or agreeing them through consultation? If the second, who do you involve? Here are seven methods by which to agree priorities. They involve four different, sometimes overlapping, styles of decision-making: tell, sell, consult and collaborate.

Do-it-yourself	The senior/middle manager knows most of the problems and can therefore identify priorities.
Sales talk	The senior/middle manager identifies priorities, and tries to sell them to the staff.
Phone-in	The priorities are presented, but staff are also invited to give their views.
Foot-in-the-door	Tentatively suggest priorities; if accepted, then carry on, but be ready to change the proposed priorities if necessary.
The buck stops here	Present the priorities, gather alternative proposals, but make the final decision.
Arms length	Encourage the staff to decide, but within certain limits.
The staff decides	The senior manager assigns full responsibility to the staff, who decide the priorities.

Are there really *four* styles?

- Tell

- Sell

- Consult

- Join

Changing priorities

Setting priorities is a flexible business. Priorities can change. A priority identified at the start of planning may be more or less important as time goes on and circumstances alter.

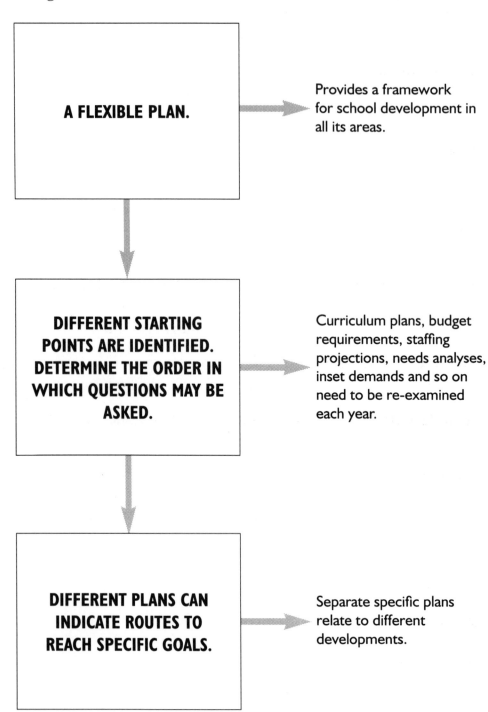

A FLEXIBLE PLAN.

Provides a framework for school development in all its areas.

DIFFERENT STARTING POINTS ARE IDENTIFIED. DETERMINE THE ORDER IN WHICH QUESTIONS MAY BE ASKED.

Curriculum plans, budget requirements, staffing projections, needs analyses, inset demands and so on need to be re-examined each year.

DIFFERENT PLANS CAN INDICATE ROUTES TO REACH SPECIFIC GOALS.

Separate specific plans relate to different developments.

Selecting a priority and thinking about action

Having related priorities to your aims and values and considered what other people think, you can **finalize your priorities**.

First, organize for selecting priorities	**Second, prepare for action**
↓	↓

What alternative priorities are there?	Who needs to be involved with your chosen priority?
What resources would be needed for each?	How can you schedule all the activities required by the plan?
Who needs to be involved in deciding between these priorities?	How can the resources be found at each stage?
Which is the most important priority?	

Being ready for the unexpected

You must always be ready for unforeseen events and be able to respond to them quickly and effectively. You may have to review the policies, strategies and tactics decided upon.

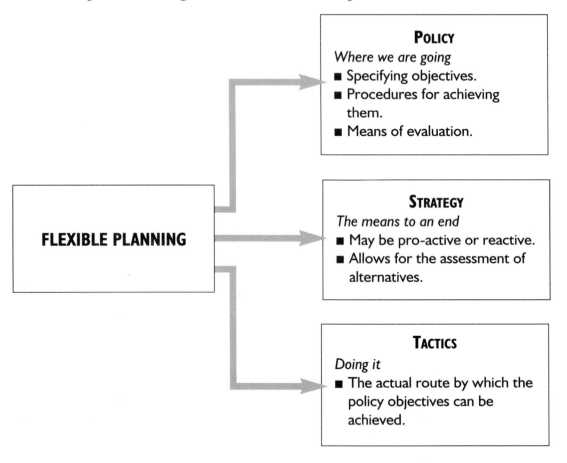

FLEXIBLE PLANNING

POLICY
Where we are going
- Specifying objectives.
- Procedures for achieving them.
- Means of evaluation.

STRATEGY
The means to an end
- May be pro-active or reactive.
- Allows for the assessment of alternatives.

TACTICS
Doing it
- The actual route by which the policy objectives can be achieved.

Are you being successful?

How will you know that you have been successful? Do not fall into the trap of thinking that dealing with an issue you have identified as a priority will be the sole indicator of success. Your criteria for gauging success must take into account other factors, for example:
- Have other priorities been considered and allowed for?
- Have you been flexible?

4 *Carrying out an audit: where are you now?*

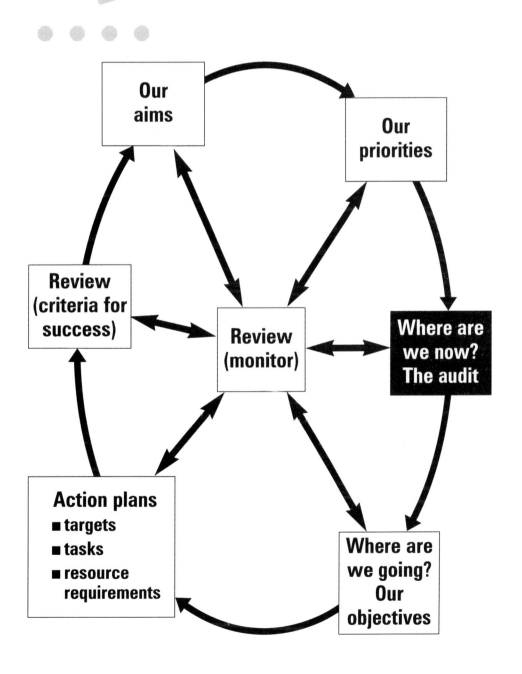

What is an audit?

In education, an **audit** is a means by which a school's current situation, or some aspect of it, can be described, recorded and understood in a systematic way using a variety of techniques. The information gathered can be used to decide:

■ what the school's current strengths and weaknesses are;
■ what opportunities exist for improvement;
■ what threats to such improvement are apparent.

What makes a good audit?

A good audit uses what happened before and what is happening now as a guide to future action. It is based on information that

■ is of sufficient quality;
■ provides an accurate picture of the school;
■ is drawn from a representative cross-section of those involved with the school;
■ acknowledges different points of view;
■ is obtained through a variety of techniques.

A successful audit depends on

■ the techniques used to collect the information;
■ the methods used to interpret it.

The audit

The audit enables you to discover and appraise those factors which affect and influence the school's performance. It entails a fair amount of listening. You need to sound out opinions, learn from other people's experiences and appreciate their perceptions and ideas for future improvements. A successful audit can provide support for your aims and help you to develop action plans which specify clear objectives and targets.

Here are four methods which together form a comprehensive audit:

METHOD 1: 'Swot' analysis

What are our STRENGTHS?

What are our WEAKNESSES?

What OPPORTUNITIES are available?

What THREATS are apparent?

Often a very simple grid analysis or questionnaire can be very successful.

METHOD 2: *A staff discussion document*

	What are we doing well?	What could we be doing better?	Have we any unused potential?
What are we doing now?			
How are we doing it?			
How are we responding to the environment in which we work?			
What are the responses and reactions of other people?			

METHOD 3: *Client satisfaction*

A pupil responds

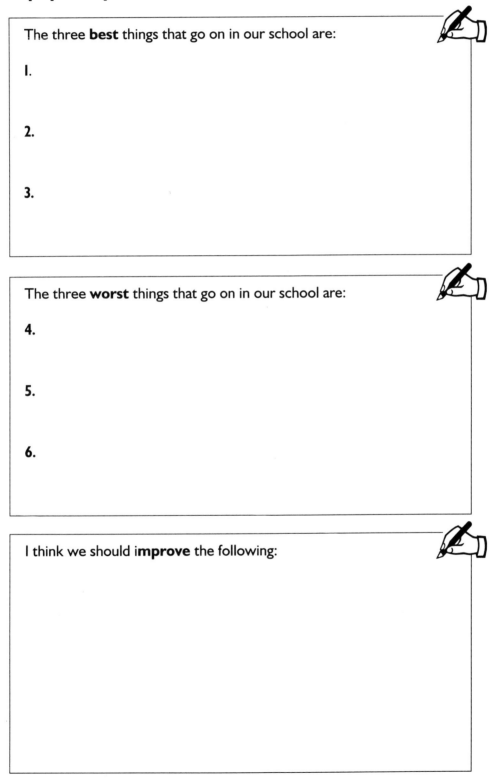

The three **best** things that go on in our school are:

1.

2.

3.

The three **worst** things that go on in our school are:

4.

5.

6.

I think we should **improve** the following:

A parent responds

The three **best** things about the school are:

1.

2.

3.

The three **worst** things about the school are:

4.

5.

6.

What I would most like to see **changed** in the school is:

METHOD 4: A 'just a tick' survey

Take, for example

Setting up a health education audit

This is a simple audit procedure within a specified curriculum area.

The following is taken from the *Exeter Survey Health Behaviour Questionnaire*.

Some minor modifications have been made to the original.

Setting up a health education audit

'There is good evidence for believing that a considerable amount of health related teaching goes on in most schools. It would be of considerable benefit to discover what is being attempted and when such teaching occurs.' (SCHEP, 1984)

Using the list of topics taken from the 'Just a Tick' survey staff can be asked to indicate what health education is going on in their class/subject. This information can be used by the *Co-ordinator* to plot a grid showing the school's current provision of health education.

The exercise needs some preliminary introduction to make it understandable. It could be introduced at a *Staff* or *Heads of Department* meeting.

Although the inquiry is most useful in indicating coverage and organization across and throughout the curriculum, a limited exercise which centres upon selected areas is possible, such as *Biology, Home Economics, Physical Education, Religious Education* and *English*.

The whole school grid can be used as a basis for discussion on curriculum development. Some of the following questions might result from the curriculum review:

- Do there appear to be significant gaps in particular years?
- Do certain years receive little or no coverage of health education topics?
- Is there a particular subject/department carrying the bulk of the work?
- Does there appear to be duplication by different subjects in the same year?
- Is provision *'developmental'*?
  and
- How might the provision be improved?

To: Class Teacher/Head of Year/Head of Department

On the proforma, please would you indicate the coverage given on the topics listed. It would be useful if you could use the following code letters if the categories they represent give a fair indication of the way in which the topic is treated.

A a systematic course of study to **all pupils**.
B a systematic course of study to **some pupils**.
C no course of study but work on the topic is **certain to arise**.
D no course of study but work on the topic **may arise**.

Here's a fragment of a sample return from a *Biologist*:

	School years				
	7	8	9	10	11
1 How the body works	A	A	A	B	B
2 Staying well		A			
3 Immunization		A	B		B
4 Illness and recovery					
5 Talking with doctors, nurses, dentists					
6 Care of hair, teeth, skin					
7 Care of eyes		C			

There will be overlap between topics, indeed some topics may appear to include others. Given this limitation the information will help to compile a profile of current *Health Education* provision: where topics are taught in the curriculum, to whom they are taught and whether they are planned or incidental.

If there is other work that you do which you consider to be obviously health related, please add the topic(s) to the list and indicate the degree of coverage you give to it (them).

Teacher/Department

Topic	School years				
	7	8	9	10	11
1 How the body works					
2 Staying well					
3 Immunization					
4 Illness and recovery					
5 Talking with doctors, nurses, dentists					
6 Care of hair, teeth, skin					
7 Care of eyes					
8 Care of feet					
9 Human reproduction					
10 Menstruation (periods)					
11 Food and health					
12 Drinking alcohol					
13 Glue sniffing and drugs					
14 Smoking					
15 Physical fitness					
16 Understanding the needs of people with disabilities					
17 Understanding the needs of elderly people					
18 Health and social services					
19 Safety at home					
20 Safety in traffic					
21 Water safety					
22 First aid					
23 Family life					
24 Separation from parents					
25 Death and bereavement					

	School years				
	7	8	9	10	11
26 Stress and relaxation					
27 The difference between boys' and girls' behaviour					
28 Physical growth and development					
29 Relationships with other boys and girls of the same age					
30 Understanding people of different race or religion					
31 Feelings (love, hate, anger, jealousy)					
32 Bullying					
33 Building self-confidence					
34 Making decisions					
35 Honesty					
36 Responsibility for your own behaviour					
37 Spare-time activities					
38 Boredom					
39 Caring for pets					
40 Vandalism					
41 Stealing					
42 Pollution					
43 Conservation					
44 Contraception					
45 Parenthood and child care					
46 Sexually transmitted diseases/HIV and AIDS					
47 Control of body weight					
48 Violence on television					
49 Cancer					

5 *Your objectives: where are you going?*

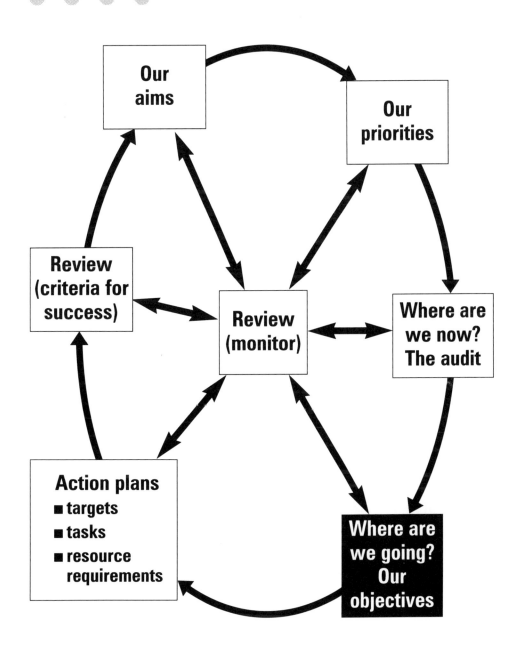

Our aims

Our priorities

Review (criteria for success)

Review (monitor)

Where are we now? The audit

Action plans
- targets
- tasks
- resource requirements

Where are we going? Our objectives

Why objectives are important

An objective is a precise, measurable statement of intended outcomes. These outcomes specify intentions rather than actions.

Setting objectives is important because objectives

- give clarity of purpose;
- establish the central task;
- go beyond the day to day;
- provide guidelines for development;
- set standards for assessment.

How do these apply to *your* school?

Setting objectives

To set objectives, you need to clarify the issue involved.

What factors are causing concern?

Who feels that it *is* a concern?

What will happen if nothing is done?

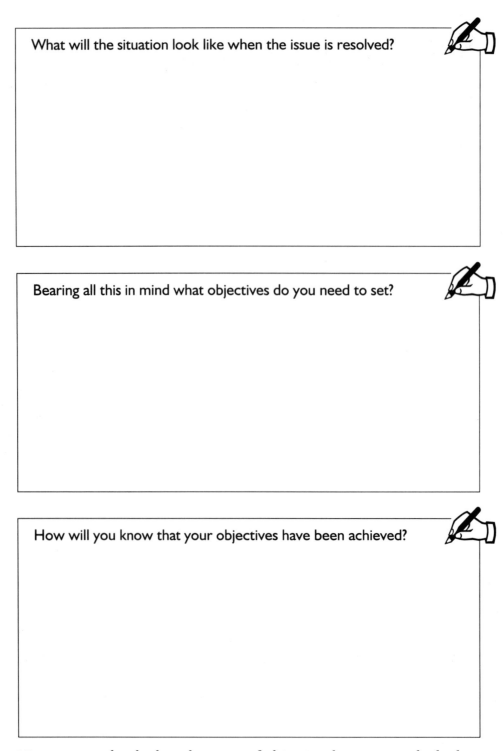

What will the situation look like when the issue is resolved?

Bearing all this in mind what objectives do you need to set?

How will you know that your objectives have been achieved?

Now you need to look at the types of objective that exist, and which you need to set yourselves.

Types of objective

There are two main types of objective.

1 Output objectives

■ Focus on day-to-day results
 e.g. routine planning and procedures, including examination
 arrangements.

2 Change objectives

■ Focus on the short-term or long-term changes you want to make.

Are your objectives for change aimed at achieving:

■ **more**

■ **better**

■ **different**

results?

Writing objectives

Your planning will improve if you can

- precisely specify your objectives;
- identify your criteria for success.

Make sure that the objectives you write down

- are precise;
- indicate the result required;
- are realistic;
- are measurable.

For example

Objective	Is it precise?	Does it indicate the results required?	Is it realistic?	Is it measurable?
To reduce absenteeism by 80%	✓ yes	✓ yes	? almost certainly not	✓ yes
To reduce absenteeism by 10%	✓ yes	✓ yes	✓ probably yes	✓ yes
To improve the school ethos	✗ no	? not really	? not expressed like this	? not really

You also need to identify the criteria for success at the same time as you write down your objectives. Your success in reducing absenteeism by a specific amount is actually achieving the target set. However, your success in improving the school ethos may be harder to confirm unless you can agree criteria which you know you can measure (see also Chapter 7 Reviewing success: what criteria to use).

Action plans: targets, tasks and resources

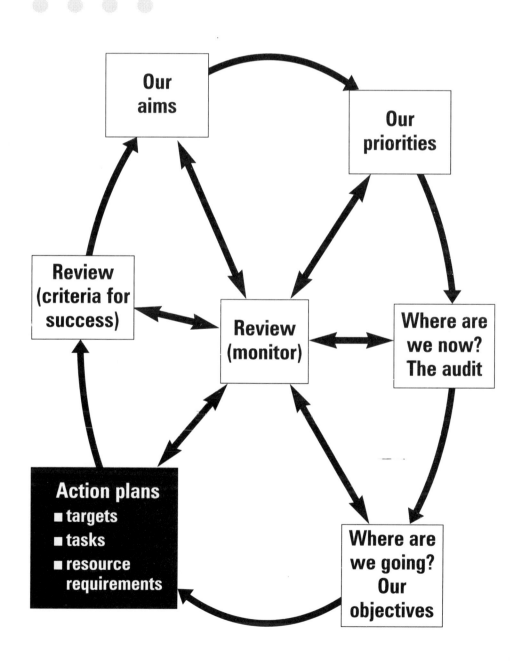

Our aims

Our priorities

Review (criteria for success)

Review (monitor)

Where are we now? The audit

Action plans
- targets
- tasks
- resource requirements

Where are we going? Our objectives

What is a plan?

An action plan sets out the targets and tasks which are designed to help you achieve your objectives. Action planning maps out the way you are going to get things done.

Planning:

- uses past experiences to build on successes and to learn from mistakes;
- establishes short-term objectives as stepping stones to long-term goals;
- increases professional awareness of key issues;
- organizes and schedules daily work;
- considers people and their needs alongside setting up administrative routines.

Not all plans are the same. They vary in size, timing, their use of resources, in the priority they are given and in the criteria for success that they set out.

Plans vary in size	They can be *small* e.g. improving a particular department.	They can be *large* e.g. improving the whole school environment.
Plans vary in timing	*Short-term* e.g. organizing an open day.	*Long-term* e.g. the erection of new buildings.
Plans vary in resource needs	*Minor* e.g. setting up a School Council.	*Major capital programme* e.g. new buildings.
Plans vary in the priority they have and in the success criteria they specify	*Low* e.g. improving the school grounds.	*High* e.g. Improving the school's safety record.

Defining the planning tasks

When starting on an action plan, you need to find answers to the following questions:

- Where are you going to start?
- What do you want to achieve?
- Within what time-scale do you want to achieve it?
- What decisions need to be made?
- What are your objectives?
- What are your priorities?
- What must you schedule?
- What will it cost?
- How are you going to do it?
- How do you tell others about the plan?
- What problems might there be in carrying out the plan?

Putting the plan into action requires:

- training staff;
- communicating with others;
- setting performance standards;
- targeting time, people, resources;
- motivating staff, governors, pupils, yourselves;
- evaluating objectives, outcomes, success;
- modifying the plan and your policies.

What will the plan look like?

As we have already seen, an action plan varies in size, time-scale and the resources required to carry it through. They can be based on whole-school development or on smaller, single issues which can stand alone or be incorporated into a larger whole-school development plan.

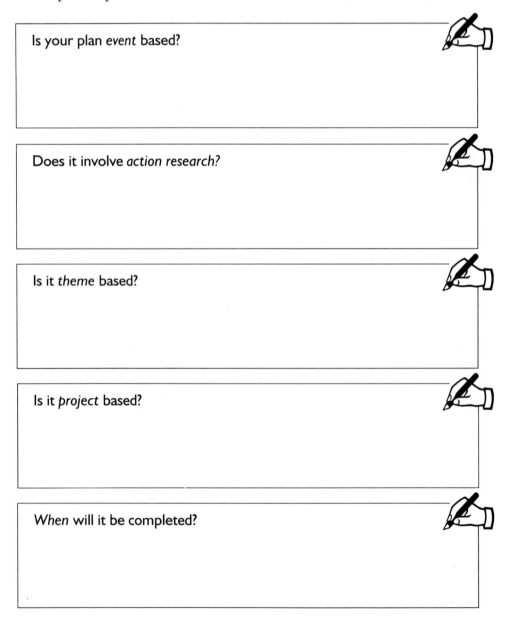

Is your plan *event* based?

Does it involve *action research*?

Is it *theme* based?

Is it *project* based?

When will it be completed?

Developing the plan

Planning for action

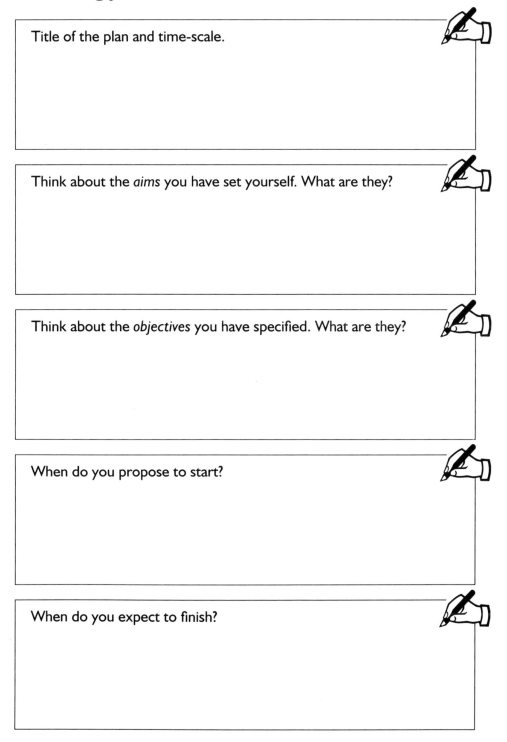

Title of the plan and time-scale.

Think about the *aims* you have set yourself. What are they?

Think about the *objectives* you have specified. What are they?

When do you propose to start?

When do you expect to finish?

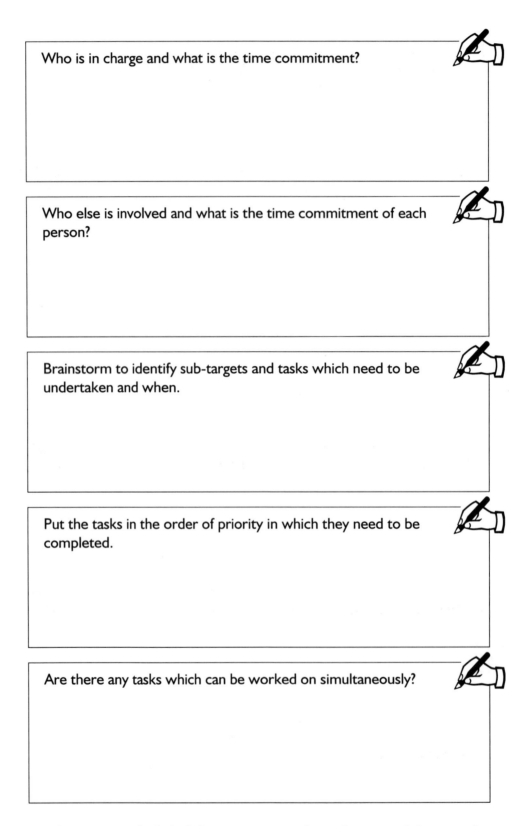

Who is in charge and what is the time commitment?

Who else is involved and what is the time commitment of each person?

Brainstorm to identify sub-targets and tasks which need to be undertaken and when.

Put the tasks in the order of priority in which they need to be completed.

Are there any tasks which can be worked on simultaneously?

You have now scheduled the necessary tasks and arranged them in the sequence required for achieving your objective.

Now communicate

You must communicate your planning arrangements to those involved in, or likely to be affected by, the developments.

	Tasks in time sequence	Intended completion date	Who is involved?	INSET needs?	Wider implic- ations?	Tick when completed and then move on
Task 1						
Task 2						
Task 3						
Task 4						

What resources are needed?

Staff: is training, professional development or personal support required?

Materials/equipment?

Books/worksheets?

Other/contingency?

Setting target dates

Once you have agreed the content of the plan you should set target dates and publish them alongside the plan. These dates will depend on

- the scope of the plan;
- the level of changes envisaged;
- the resources available to the school;
- the time available to staff and others.

You should also agree:

- how long you want the initial review to last;
- when you want the plan to be completed by.

For example

Planning	Target dates							
	Review present situation		Identify changes needed		Put changes in order of priority		Time table to implement changes	
	Start	Complete	Start	Complete	Start	Complete	Start	Complete

How to avoid surprises

Have you explained the facts and given reasons to those affected? What are they?

Have you listed the benefits objectively and without exaggeration? What are they?

Have you satisfactorily dealt with others' concerns and questions about the plan? What are they?

Have you invited participation and asked for suggestions?
What are they?

Have you encouraged and received commitment and
involvement? Who is getting involved?

Have you acknowledged the 'rough spots'? What are they?

Reviewing success: what criteria to use

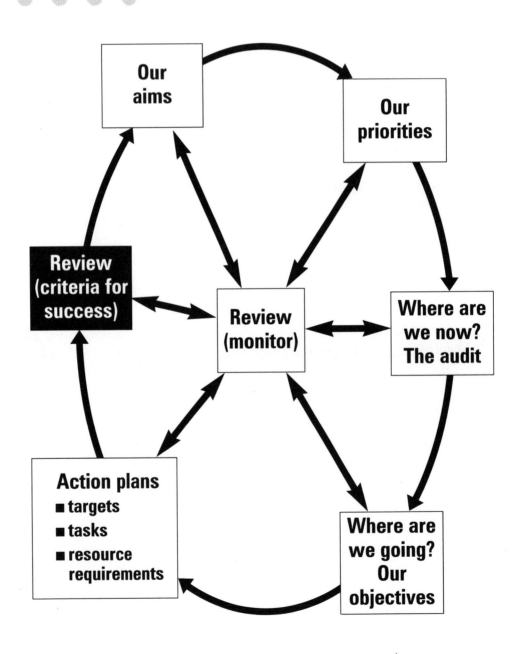

Introduction

It is essential to keep your plan under review. This section provides practical advice on how to monitor the development plan on a regular basis as you are putting it into practice; how to decide where and in what ways your plan is working and where it is not; how to rescue elements in the plan that are failing; and how to gauge success at the end of one developmental planning cycle before moving on to the next proposed cycle of development. There are two separate and distinct ways of doing this:

1 Reviewing your criteria for success

- This takes place at the end of a developmental planning cycle and assesses progress at one particular moment before moving on to a further planning cycle.
- It can be thought of as an 'end of process' or 'fixed-point' review.

2 Monitoring

- This is a continuous process of examining the emerging results of the plan as it is being carried out.

Reviewing criteria for success

An end of process or fixed-point review means

- asking yourselves where you are now;
- looking back at how you arrived there;
- deciding where you were successful;
- examining what helped and what hindered progress;
- deciding where to go next.

At the end of this review, set new clear and realistic targets for further progress.

Why is it important?

The way you review your criteria for success determines how well you perform in the next stage of the development cycle.

The review

- provides an opportunity to share information and reactions;
- enables you to model future development based on that shared experience;
- allows for public accountability and involves other people with an interest in the plan;
- offers a formal process which provides a credible structure to support future planning cycles.

How often is it necessary?

It is up to you. Fixed-point reviews are likely to be more frequent at the start of a fresh initiative and less so as the development matures, for example a termly review moving to an annual one.

Where an overall school development plan is supported by a series of smaller department plans, it does not make sense to review all the departmental plans at the same time. Managing fixed-point reviews requires scheduling.

Here is an example of part of a schedule for one school:

INITIATIVE	DEPARTMENT MANAGER	SEP	OCT	NOV	DEC	JAN	FEB	MAR	APR	MAY	JUNE	JULY	AUG
Whole school development plan	Head									*			
Staffing	Head									*			
Curriculum	Department Head Curriculum		*										
Careers guidance	Head of Department Careers								*				
Staff development	Department Head Staff Development							*					
Assessment recording achievement	Department Head Staff Development				*								

Schedule of fixed-point reviews for Norham Community High School.

Helpful hints

1 Key decisions to be made when setting up the fixed-point review

Department, theme, subject or area to be evaluated?

How? What process will you use?

When?

What will you gather
information about?

Over what period?

Who will you involve:

Teachers?

Other adults?

Pupils?

2 Getting information for the fixed-point review

You will need to consider how you will gather information which tells you how far you are meeting your success criteria.

Here are *three* possible methods:

Method 1: Monitoring the 'actual happening'

On a day-to-day basis, you will monitor what is actually happening whilst your evaluation is underway. What will you monitor?

Method 2: Monitoring the fixed-point, the 'snapshot'

When will you take
the snapshot?

How will you set it up?

What elements will
you try to catch?

How long will the
time exposure be?

Will the snapshot be
totally *internal* or will
it be *external* too?

Method 3: Monitoring through dialogue and support, and by 'feedback'

Things to think about:

Will you use a mentor or critical friend?

Will you recognize the importance of feelings?

Will you get people to talk about their intentions?

Will you replay the events, in order to get people to think reflectively?

3 Documenting your review

A record of the review should be kept. The record might look like this:

First review

People involved ....
....
....
....

Date of review ....

On balance, did you succeed more

than you failed? .... Yes/No

What factors helped you towards success? ....
....
....
....

First review
continued

What problems/difficulties prevented success? ....

....

....

....

....

How can these be overcome? ....

....

....

....

....

Future actions? ....

....

....

....

....

Suggested re-defined target and date? ....

....

....

....

....

Agreed re-defined target and date? ....

....

....

....

....

Monitoring: reviewing how well things are going

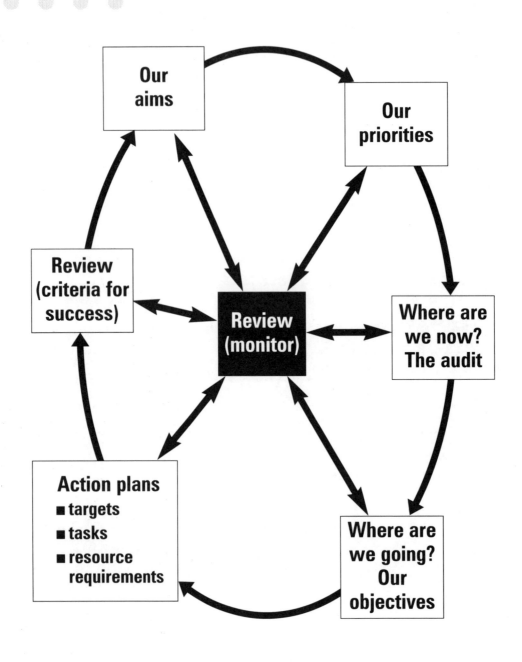

Monitoring is the second aspect of reviewing. It is the continuous process of examining the emerging results of your plan as you carry it out. This is at the heart of successful developmental planning.

Why is it important?

There is often no specific time set aside during the school year to monitor how development is progressing and yet there is little point in waiting until the end of a school year to discover if you are achieving your objectives. Monitoring can offer the following benefits:

- you can find out if the plan is working and how well;
- you know if you are making progress towards your objectives;
- you can assess if the required standards are being reached;
- you are able to take corrective action to meet or maintain the standards you have set within the time-scale agreed;
- you can identify individuals who are under pressure and allocate or redirect resources to alleviate areas of stress.

What do you monitor?

You need to monitor each stage of your developmental planning, assessing what progress you have made and introducing changes in the light of different circumstances.

Monitor:

- Aims
  Are they clearly defined and agreed?
  Do they incorporate a 'mission statement'?
- Priorities
  Which are becoming more urgent aspects of development?
  Are they long-term or short-term? High or low cost?
- Objectives
  Are these still appropriate?
  Are they specific enough, measurable, attainable, realistic or time limited?
- The audit
  In the light of the audit, do you need to amend any aims, priorities, objectives and so on?

Monitor the action plans:

- Targets
  Are they still attainable?
  Is the time-scale right?
  Do you need new targets?
- Tasks
  Are they helping you to achieve your targets?
  Would different tasks be more effective?
  Do you need to introduce new tasks?
- Resources
  Were your initial assumptions correct about the resources you need and what is available to you?
  Do you require different resources which you had not anticipated?
  Who has become involved in this development?
  Do other people now need to be brought in as well?

Monitor your criteria for success:

Are they still appropriate?
What evidence will show you how you are doing?
Are you moving towards success with the indicators you have specified?
Are there other indicators that would do the job better?

How do you monitor?

1 Use a mentor

Appoint a mentor, preferably someone who is not too close to what you are doing but whose judgement you respect. The mentor can ask you the critical and sometimes painful questions which will alert you to the need to check your progress.

2 Schedule monitoring into the process

Build monitoring into the development process by timetabling it in at each stage. Decide when you will carry out each kind of review and what criteria for success you will evaluate (see also Reviewing criteria for success page 65).

3 Seek extra feedback

Monitor what is happening through discussions with other people.

- How did each activity or strategy work out?
- How do you feel about each activity?
- How do other people – colleagues, governors, parents and pupils – feel about each activity?
- Were the resources used effectively?
- Encourage the people you work with to reflect on and, where necessary, reconsider their position at each stage of the developmental planning process.

9 Involving others

Governors, parents, pupils and employers

Governors in schools now have much greater responsibilities to cope with. Parents ask more searching questions about the way the school works and how their children are getting on. Pupils themselves increasingly want to know too. Employers want closer involvement with their local schools. All of them can benefit from understanding and, where appropriate, being a part of the process of developmental planning.

A school that embarks on developmental planning can produce leaflets specifically for their governors, parents, pupils and local employers which explain what developmental planning is all about and the advantages that can come from its successful introduction and development.

Here are two examples of a leaflet which sets out the basic model of developmental planning and the benefits to be gained for those involved in running the school. Although they are aimed at parents and pupils, they can be adapted for other interested groups, such as governors and employers.

A parent's guide to developmental planning

Many parents will want to ask searching questions about the way the school works and what precisely it does for their children.

So what we've tried to do here is to provide answers to some of the most frequent questions which come up in conversation.

The simple answer is that we want to improve on what we do already. We aren't totally satisfied with what goes on now.

But there are other reasons: the Education Acts of 1988 and 1993, the introduction of the National Curriculum with assessment and testing and the changes brought about by GCSE and local management of schools (LMS).

The main change we need is to improve the way we go about planning what we do. The rate at which things happen nowadays means that we *have* to change our planning in order to survive.

Developmental planning is a way of creating a plan of action. It is a process that becomes a valuable tool for all of us – teachers, pupils and parents – to use.

Most people, at one time or another, whether they work in business, industry or school, use developmental planning to work out *what* needs to be done, *how* to do it and by *when*.

> *Right, very interesting, but how does it work in practice?*

What we have done to answer this question is to show you the planning model which has been worked out to help us:

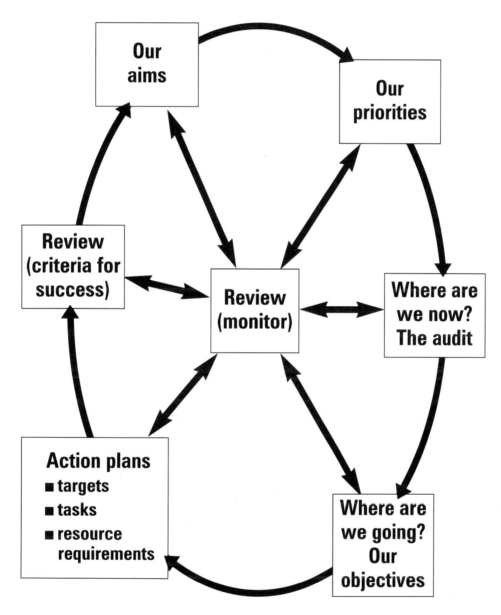

Basically, we start by finding out what the situation is, next we sort out our plans and then take the necessary action.

And you will notice that we keep everything under constant review so that if things go wrong we can act quickly and effectively.

> *Yes, that's all very well, but what's so special about developmental planning?*

Well, there are some really good reasons for this. Developmental planning scores well because:

- it focuses attention on the importance of the education of each individual pupil;

- it brings together all the different sorts of decisions we make, finance management, resources and learning approaches;

- it gives us a technique which we can work long-term and short-term;

- it provides the sort of support which teachers and students need in coping with pressures;

- it encourages only the changes which make a real contribution to education;

- it improves the quality of our own educational provision and provides new skills;

- it emphasizes teachers in partnership with children, governors, and of course with *you*;

- it allows the school to monitor, evaluate and report on what it is doing at any particular moment with minimum fuss.

And you will have realized that what we have just been talking about is

---

providing a high quality education service

---

and *you* are an essential partner in that.

So here is the final question we hope to hear you asking:

> *Can I get involved as a parent?*

The fact is that your involvement is crucial to everything we do.

We are constantly looking out for support and help, so if you want to make a bigger contribution let us know what you have in mind.

But even if you don't get too involved 'up-front' you can still provide massive help by taking a strong interest in how your children are getting on and talking to them about the benefits of being at this school.

A pupil's guide to developmental planning

As you go through school, you will need to have some clear idea about where you are going in your school work, when you are outside school, in your future career and in your life generally.

What is on your mind at the moment:

- completing your homework?
- organizing your subject choices?
- getting fit?
- deciding on your future career?
- saving up for a holiday?

Planning for these things gives you a better chance of achieving what *you* want.

Developmental planning is a way of creating a plan of action to help you make the right decisions and know how best to carry them out. It is a valuable tool in working out *what* needs to be done, *how* to do it and by *when*.

Planning helps to keep people on target. For example, you can use this approach

- for your personal development plan, to cover your lesson targets, examinations and career plans;
- for your own or your group's plan to make sure a technology project reaches its completion stage;
- for a class or school in planning to stage a drama or musical production.

It can also help you to have a say in making our school run better and in deciding what goes on.

A developmental plan uses words like

- aims   - priorities   - objectives
- action plans   - reviewing   - monitoring.

Here is what developmental planning looks like as a diagram:

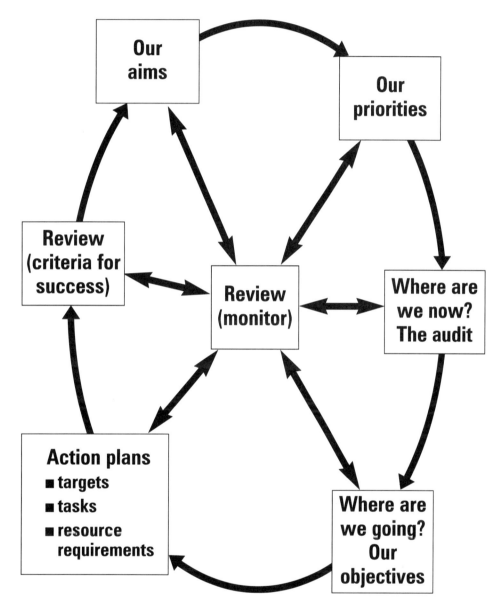

You can start anywhere in this planning wheel, although you must always ask yourself 'How am I getting on?'. This is so important that we have put this question at the centre of the wheel, see 'Review (monitor)'.

Your teacher can explain the planning wheel in more detail.

Your own personal development plan

My aims:

My priorities:

Where am I now? What point am I starting from?

Where am I going? What do I want to achieve?

How am I going to do it? What are my action plans?

Will I need extra help and more time, people to help me, equipment to help me?

Am I going to set a date by which time I will have achieved my target?

How will I have decided whether I have succeeded in, say, 12 months?

How often do I need to check whether I am on course?

DATE: .... SIGNATURE: ....

Appendices:

MODEL ONE

Development plan for:

Date of initial submission:

TITLE: _____

MANAGER: _____ **DATE:** _____

Our aims	Where are we now?

Our priorities	Where are we going?

Action plans

Target one
Date:

Tasks:

Resources:

Criteria for success:

Target two
Date:

Tasks:

Resources:

Criteria for success:

The Whole Curriculum Issues Project Developmental Planning Model

A glossary of terms

Development plan A map of the most suitable route to get to where the school, or department, wants to be.

Aims The long-term goals, based on the school's values and philosophy, which transcend all other, shorter-term or minor goals.

Priority Giving greater or lesser weight to specific aims over the period for which you are planning.

Audit A way to describe, record and understand the current situation using a variety of techniques.

Objectives Precise and measurable statements of intended outcomes which specify intentions rather than actions.

Action plan A programme which sets out targets and tasks designed to help you achieve your objectives.

Target A timed element within the programme.

Task A specific job to be carried out within the time imposed by the target.

Resource Material and support which generates a cost in terms of time, human energy or other materials.

Review (monitor) A continuous process of examining the emerging results of the plan as it is being carried out.

Review (criteria for success) An end-of-process review leading to the next development cycle.

For further information on this approach to planning please contact: Whole Curriculum Issues Project Manager, Norham Community High School, Alnwick Avenue, North Shields, NE29 7BU.

Development plan for:

Health Education

Date of initial submission: | *14th December*

TITLE: *Health Education*
MANAGER: *Mr T D Lewis*

DATE: *14th December*

Our aims

1 To provide facilities which enable children to follow a healthy lifestyle in school.
2 To develop a whole-school approach towards Health Education within and outside the structured curriculum.
3 To promote an environment which is sensitive and responsive to the emotional needs of children.
4 To promote knowledge and understanding of factors affecting physical health.
5 To develop understanding of the needs of others and to foster responsible and caring attitudes towards others.
6 To promote environmental awareness and to assist in responding to community needs.

Where are we now?

1 Health Education topics are being addressed in a number of curriculum areas but with no cross-curricular co-ordination of content, context, timing or use of resources.
2 There have been few whole-school activities specifically planned to promote Health Education.
3 North Tyneside LEA has issued a Health Education Policy and guidelines.
4 HMIs have issued recommendation for cross-curricular Health Education (Curriculum Matters Series).
5 Individuals have expressed concern for the unhealthy diet of many pupils at lunchtime.

Our priorities

1 To negotiate a school HEALTH EDUCATION POLICY.
2 To provide facilities to encourage children to choose a healthy diet in school.
3 To explore the extent to which HEALTH EDUCATION topics are presently being addressed within the structured curriculum.

Where are we going?

1 A school Health Education Policy is to be developed by the Science and Health Canton, in negotiation with the Headteacher, Governors, LEA Adviser and all staff.
2 A 'just a tick' audit of Health Education topics presently being addressed within the structured curriculum is to be made throughout all cantons.
3 A more detailed audit of topics will then follow to analyse content, teaching methods, terms taught and resources used for each year group in Health Education.
4 Present Health Education provision will be reviewed in its effectiveness to meet the policy aims of the school.
5 Inadequacies and duplication within Health Education topics will be addressed within priorities.
6 School meals will be improved in dietary balance and the dining room environment will be improved.

Action plans

Target one
Date: 7th March

To negotiate a school Health Education Policy which meets the approval of teachers, governors and the LEA.

Tasks:
1 Analysis of LEA and HMI recommendations.
2 Identify Statements of Attainment related to Health Education (Science NC).
3 Circulate draft policy for whole school discussion and feedback.
4 Prepare final draft policy.
5 Agenda policy for approval at governors' meeting.

Resources:
1 Duplication of initial draft and final draft policies.
2 Meeting time for discussion at department, canton and whole staff, and governors' meetings.
3 LEA, HMI and National Curriculum documentation.

Criteria for success:
Final policy for Health Education within the school is approved by staff, governors and LEA.

Target two
Date: 12th April

To organize a whole school 'Healthy Eating Week' (12th-16th March).
To include:
■ a new school menu;
■ a re-arrangement of the dining room and its procedures;
■ an awareness-raising with pupils, parents and staff;
■ a curricular contribution from departments to the theme of the week.

Tasks:
1 Arrange meeting with head school meals adviser, cook and other staff, to discuss menus.
2 Review dining room arrangements and procedures.
3 Prepare campaign booklets.
4 Request department inputs.
5 Publicity in schools and social press.
6 Organize competition for pupils.
7 Produce programme of related activities.

Resources:
1 Meeting time for task one.
2 Materials for booklets, posters, badges etc.
3 Time for preparation of tasks 3, 5 and 7.
4 Assembly time for awareness-raising.

Criteria for success:
Results of competition and observation indicate that children are choosing a healthier diet. New arrangements meet with pupils' and staff approval.

The Whole Curriculum Issues Project Developmental Planning Model

A glossary of terms

Development plan   A map of the most suitable route to get to where the school, or department, wants to be.

Aims   The long-term goals, based on the school's values and philosophy, which transcend all other, shorter-term or minor goals.

Priority   Giving greater or lesser weight to specific aims over the period for which you are planning.

Audit   A way to describe, record and understand the current situation using a variety of techniques.

Objectives   Precise and measurable statements of intended outcomes which specify intentions rather than actions.

Action plan   A programme which sets out targets and tasks designed to help you achieve your objectives.

Target   A timed element within the programme.

Task   A specific job to be carried out within the time imposed by the target.

Resource   Material and support which generates a cost in terms of time, human energy or other materials.

Review (monitor)   A continuous process of examining the emerging results of the plan as it is being carried out.

Review (criteria for success)   An end-of-process review leading to the next development cycle.

For further information on this approach to planning please contact: Whole Curriculum Issues Project Manager, Norham Community High School, Alnwick Avenue, North Shields, NE29 7BU.

Development plan for:

School Plan Overview

Date of initial submission: | *3rd February* |

TITLE: *Whole School Development Plan*
MANAGER: *Norham Community High School* **DATE**: *3rd February*

Our aims

The school development plans are produced in a format which is more accessible and readily understood by
■ teachers;
■ LEA;
■ school governors.
The school development plans will comprise of
■ a school development plan which will briefly refer to major developmental requirements of the school;
■ mini development plans which will identify specific areas of development e.g. curriculum and finance.

Where are we now?

Audit...

1 The following groups have been involved in in-service training for developmental planning:
■ senior management;
■ cross-curricular working group;
■ technology planning group.
2 There is still a need to raise awareness of the need for forward planning with both staff and governors.
3 Newcastle Polytechnic, North Tyneside TVEI and Norham High School are involved in a project which is intended to facilitate the production of development planning models.
4 Examples of planning models are available from the Curricular Issues Project Manager.

Our priorities

1 To agree the School Development Plan with
■ senior management;
■ governors.
2 To involve relevant staff and where appropriate school governors with the construction of the mini plans.
3 To ensure that all appropriate parties including parents understand the developmental plans of the school.

Where are we going?

Objectives...

1 It is intended to produce the main and mini development plans by June 1990.
2 The main development plan will consist of
■ whole school aims   ■ priorities   ■ audit
■ objectives   ■ action plans   ■ review procedures.
3 The following mini development plans will be produced:
1 Role and staffing.
2 Curriculum.
3 Management structure including Canton and Pastoral, including allowance, structure and job descriptions.
4 Special educational needs
5 Assessment and recording achievement.
6 Schemes of work and programmes of study.
7 Arrangements for reporting to parents and governors.
8 Departmental and school review arrangements including review of aims and objectives.
9 Cross-curricular themes, dimensions and skills.
10 Arrangements for act of worship and RE.
11 Multi-cultural and equal opportunities.
12 Industrial liaison.
13 Community development.
14 Finance and resource management.
15 Staff development.
16 Liaison with LEA, parents, school governors and school brochure.
17 Cross-phase liaison.
18 Rolling programme of fabric enhancement.

Action plans

Target one

Date: 23rd April

To raise awareness with staff and governors regarding the requirements of the school development plan.

Tasks:

1 Prepare a one hour briefing, to take place during the one day April in-service which will outline the development plan format for the school.
2 Invite governors and school adviser to the in-service day.
3 Hold meeting with Canton co-ordinators to outline development plan model.

Resources: (including INSET)

1 Outlines of school development plans available for all staff.

Criteria for success:

1 All staff and governors understand the need for development planning.
2 The model format is understood and accepted by all parties.

Target two

Date: 15th June

To construct school and mini development plans with regard to all areas outlined in the Objectives section.

Tasks:

1 Senior management to identify areas of responsibility with regard to development plans.
2 Individual staff and governors are informed of the planning requirements.
3 Completion of provisional plans by 1st June.
4 Completion of plans by 15th June.

Resources: (including INSET)

1 All meeting time available to develop the plans.

Criteria for success:

1 All major and mini development plans are completed by the appropriate dates.
2 The plans are readily understood and clearly identify the planning needs of the schools.
3 The whole staff and governing body have a clear understanding of
■ the need for planning;
■ the alternative ways forward and the priorities which have been identified;
■ that the organizational climate is responsive to the future needs and plans of the school.

The Whole Curriculum Issues Project Developmental Planning Model

A glossary of terms

Development plan   A map of the most suitable route to get to where the school, or department, wants to be.

Aims   The long-term goals, based on the school's values and philosophy, which transcend all other, shorter-term or minor goals.

Priority   Giving greater or lesser weight to specific aims over the period for which you are planning.

Audit   A way to describe, record and understand the current situation using a variety of techniques.

Objectives   Precise and measurable statements of intended outcomes which specify intentions rather than actions.

Action plan   A programme which sets out targets and tasks designed to help you achieve your objectives.

Target   A timed element within the programme.

Task   A specific job to be carried out within the time imposed by the target.

Resource   Material and support which generates a cost in terms of time, human energy or other materials.

Review (monitor)   A continuous process of examining the emerging results of the plan as it is being carried out.

Review (criteria for success)   An end-of-process review leading to the next development cycle.

For further information on this approach to planning please contact: Whole Curriculum Issues Project Manager, Norham Community High School, Alnwick Avenue, North Shields, NE29 7BU.

SAMPLE THREE

Development plan for:

Cross Curricular
Themes, Dimensions and Skills

Date of initial submission: | *12th June*

TITLE: *Cross Curricular – Themes, Dimensions and Skills*
MANAGER: *FM Redpath*   **DATE:** *12th June*

Our aims

To ensure that all pupils experience learning in Health Education, Careers Education and Guidance, IT, Industrial and Economic Education, Citizenship, Environmental Education and to ensure that equal opportunities, multi-cultural considerations and special educational needs pervade the curriculum.

Where are we now?

1 Themes Manager's position and remit clarified.
2 LEA Health Policy received.
3 NCC documents on whole curriculum and Industrial and Economic Awareness received. IT statutory and non-statutory guidance.
4 Teachers responsible for Health, MCEO, PSE, Careers, IT SSS, Industrial Liaison, SEN in post.
5 Themes budget allocated for year.

Our priorities

1 Awareness-raising of all staff with respect to cross-curricular issues through publications and other information.
2 Working with staff responsible for Dimensions, Themes and Skills to delineate their responsibilities and support systems.

Where are we going?

1 Job description to be registered with all responsible staff.
2 Programmes of action to be agreed for Health, IT, Equal Opportunities, Multi-cultural Education, Careers, SEN, Industrial and Economic Understanding.
3 Resources to be allocated to responsible staff.
4 Arrangements for review to be negotiated with responsible staff.
5 Integrate other Themes as the NCC publishes them.

Action plans

Target one

Date: To negotiate job description with responsible staff by 20th July.

Tasks:

1 Obtain outline job description from SM.
2 Talk with all staff individually.
3 Submit negotiated job descriptions to SM.

Resources:

1 Outline job descriptions.
2 Meeting time.

Criteria for success:

That job descriptions are negotiated and accepted by all involved, including SM.

Target two

Date:

To negotiate programme of action with managers by 20th July.

Tasks:

1 Meet with each individual with prior briefing and agree programme.
2 Submit programmes to SM.

Resources:

1 Meeting time.
2 Briefing notes.
3 Outline programmes of action.

Criteria for success:

That programmes are acceptable to all.

Target three

Date: To allocate resources to managers by 30th June.

Tasks:

1 Formulate bid form.
2 Meet with all managers in committee to decide priorities.
3 Submit priorities and suggested allocation to SM.

Resources:

1 Outline bid form.
2 Meeting time.

Criteria for success:

That all agree to allocation.

Target four

Date:

To arrange a review by 10th December.

Tasks:

1 Meet with all managers to set format, purpose and time of review.

Resources:

Access to staff.

Criteria for success:

The Whole Curriculum Issues Project Developmental Planning Model

A glossary of terms

Development plan   A map of the most suitable route to get to where the school, or department, wants to be.

Aims   The long-term goals, based on the school's values and philosophy, which transcend all other, shorter-term or minor goals.

Priority   Giving greater or lesser weight to specific aims over the period for which you are planning.

Audit   A way to describe, record and understand the current situation using a variety of techniques.

Objectives   Precise and measurable statements of intended outcomes which specify intentions rather than actions.

Action plan   A programme which sets out targets and tasks designed to help you achieve your objectives.

Target   A timed element within the programme.

Task   A specific job to be carried out within the time imposed by the target.

Resource   Material and support which generates a cost in terms of time, human energy or other materials.

Review (monitor)   A continuous process of examining the emerging results of the plan as it is being carried out.

Review (criteria for success)   An end-of-process review leading to the next development cycle.

For further information on this approach to planning please contact: Whole Curriculum Issues Project Manager, Norham Community High School, Alnwick Avenue, North Shields, NE29 7BU.

Development plan

Planning Document

Area of development

Name of planner(s)

Date of this draft

First draft

Second draft

Final draft

Proposed scheme of action

Might be expressed as a flow chart or in text.

Overall purposes

Broad and fixed e.g. 'teach mathematics', 'implement industrial liaison programme', 'introduce NC Technology'. In essence what the development area exists to do.

Aims

More precise and detailed statements related to the overall purpose of the area of development.

Audit

The basic questions which need to be asked about resources, procedures and current activities.

Development starting points

Based on the answers to the audit questions.

MODEL THREE

Development plan title

Produced by

Date

Draft number

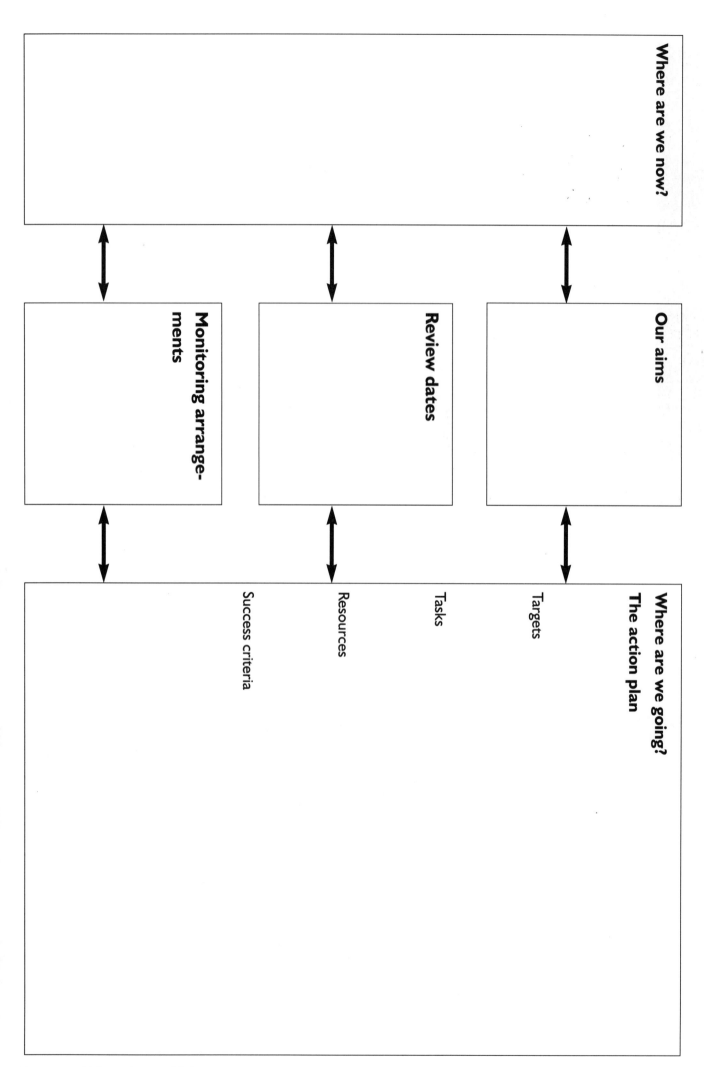

Where are we now?

Our aims

Monitoring arrange-
ments

Review dates

Where are we going?
The action plan

Targets

Tasks

Resources

Success criteria

MODEL FOUR

Plan for

Author(s)

Date

WORKING SHEET

Final purpose

Audience

General aims of subject area/theme

REVIEW

Which aims are to be dealt with specifically here?

Where are we now?

Where are we going?

REVIEW

Targets	Tasks	Reviewed by	Success criteria	
Date/Time	Date/Time	Date/Time	Date/Time	

MODEL FIVE

Development plan for:

Plan manager

Date

Our aims

Where are we now?

Aims selected for priority treatment

Where are we going?

Fixed-point review | Date

Arrangements for monitoring progress
Who:
Where:
When:

Targets	Criteria for Success	Completion date	Resources required
Target	Criteria for Success	Completion date	Resources required
Target	Criteria for Success	Completion date	Resources required
Target	Criteria for Success	Completion date	Resources required
Target	Criteria for Success	Completion date	Resources required

The WCIP Developmental Planning Model

Our aims

Our priorities

Review (criteria for success)

Review (monitor)

Where are we now? The audit

Action plans
- targets
- tasks
- resource requirements

Where are we going? Our objectives